GHOSTS' REFLECTIONS
MY CONTACT WITH
THE OTHER SIDE
BY
THE GHOST LADY

This book is non fiction
All ghost photographs were taken by The Ghost Lady

Direct all inquiries to: Ghost Lady Publishing, c/oThe Ghost Lady P.O. Box 131, Juliette Georgia. 31046
Printed in the United States of America
First Printing: October 1998
10 9 8 7 6 5 4 3 2 1

Publisher's Cataloging-in-Publication
Setran, Jodie Leigh
 Ghosts' reflections : my contact with the otherside/ by the Ghost Lady (Jodie Leigh Setran). — 1st ed.
p. Cm.— (A true ghost story and photographs ; 1)
IBSN: 0- 9665170-0-8

1. Haunted houses—Georgia.   2. Ghosts—Georgia.
3. Reincarnation.   4. Spiritualism. I. Title

BF1472.U6S48 1998   133.1'29'758576
                                          QBI8-1054

A big Thank-you to Bob for his wonderful openess and granting me the freedom to explore his previous residence. I appreciate Kathie's kindness.

To my husband John for his unconditional support. I appreciate all the encouragement from family and friends. A special thanks to Daddoo, Peti, Debra, Rhoda, Jacque, Helen, Leo, Herb, Suanne, Heidi, Rene, Sandi, Brian, Heather, Jeannie, Wehayo,Colleen, Diana and Brenda.

A very special thanks goes to Donna Licata who edited the book.

To Book Crafters: their friendly and very patient employees: Kathy, Barbara and especially Jan.

I appreciate Litho Press: Susan's kindness and her creative expertise.

Thank you-so-much to Carole Kitchens who helped me on the book.

My four loves Barnie, Oreo, Stanley and Baby "Meow."

Contents

Introduction

I call myself the Ghost Lady. My unique gift as a
clairvoyant seer has allowed me into two distinct
worlds: the living and the dead. I have sensed, heard,
smelled, and even seen those spirits who linger on in
the afterlife. I have visited haunted places and seen
many ghosts over the years. My gift has allowed me
into the ghosts' haunting world. What tragedy or
mystery kept their disembodied spirits suspended in
endless time? Why do ghosts wander around in old
places and move between different dimensions of
time?

I wanted to share my own ghost story and write
about my personnel experience that unraveled into
another whole lifetime. I met a ghost who once had
been a beautiful Southern Belle. She haunted an
antebellum mansion called Panola Hall, in Eatonton,
Georgia. The ghost remained trapped in a time that
dated back to the early 1860's.

I wrote about the ghost and her story as she had
told it to me. She had wrote names and dates leading
me to discovered the missing pieces to a past life in
which I too had onced lived during the Civil War.

Ghosts move around throughout a dense holographic atmosphere of two worlds: their world invisibled to us and our world where they had once lived. The Other Side has allowed the ghosts to come and dwell as invisible beings. Some ghosts remain trapped unable to move on. And while others choose to stay behind continually haunting places.

Ghosts choose when they want to be seen and by who. I found the camera was a resourceful tool for recording and documenting the ghosts' sightings on film. I discovered the ghosts' mystical energy fields were present in the haunted mansion's windows. The ghosts granted me permission to photograph their haunting ghostly images.

The spirit world passed on a simple message through me that we are continuously loved and supported in the afterlife. The living have not been forgotten by those who have died.

I hope my ghost story will help others to have a conscious awakening and better understanding that the spirit world and the living are connected to each other. Our words and actions toward other living beings affects our own spirit in the afterlife. Honesty gives us protection from the negative forces. The truth grants us courage to do what is right. Forgiveness sets us free and love heals all.

Sylvia coming down the stair.
Pretty Sylvia young and fair.
Oft and oft I met her there,
Smile on lip and rose in her hair.

In the distance, a woman stood in the top bedroom window holding a lantern, as she had done
many nights, over the past one hundred years, in the
haunted antebellum mansion called Panola Hall, in
Eatonton Georgia. Stormy winds blew through the
old plantation magnolia trees. Their large branches
reached out the second-story
bedroom window. The wind's howling sounded like a
woman's sorrowful weeping. Everything became
eeriely quiet when I realized the woman looking out
the mansion's window, was indeed a ghost.

The woman was infamously known by the
townsfolk as the infamous ghost called Sylvia. On
that evening, I had an eerie feeling that, perhaps, she
had found me.

Ghosts' Reflections

Ghosts stories have been told and repeated throughout many generations. The subject ghosts, wether they actually exist or are merely figments of our imagination, has been of what to me most of my life.

Ask yourself if you have ever heard strange noises creaking in the night, or had an eerie feeling someone was watching you in the darkness. You could not see or hear anything but something was there lurking in the dark. I call the eerie sensation a ghost haunting.

Death has occurred, yet ghosts are not fully aware that such an event has happened to them. Ghosts remain trapped and restless in their physical likeness, haunting places where death has been abrupt or mysterious. Their disembodied spirits appeared in vintage clothing worn during his or her lifetime.

Ghosts continue to relive certain tragic and untimely events leading up to their own death. Those disembodied spirits seek refuge in familiar places and enchanted times. Their haunted spirits continued to replay certain events over and over again.

Ghosts hold the key to unlock past secrets kept forgotten and buried deep beneath the grave. What I found was the dead communicate and helped solved their mysterious past.

The ghosts' haunted spirit attached themselves to a familiar energy field. They wander around endlessly in a timeless dimension. Energy constantly moved through windows and mirrors. Ghosts have found these two dimensional objects as open port holes to view the outside world.

Using the camera was an easy and accesible tool. I captured the ghosts floating in the mansion's haunted windows. Documenting and recording each ghost's photograph was solid proof of their existence. I do not use a camera flash for the purpose of authencity. Two types of Kodak film were used to photograph the sightings; 200 and 400 a.s.a.

My curiosity revealed the mystery leading to the Panola Hall ghost's identity and questions regarding the tragic circumstances that kept her in a timeless dimension? Who was the folklore ghost called Sylvia? What was her real name? When did she die? Why did she haunt the mansion called Panola Hall? What other secrets lurked behind the dark shadows in the haunted house? And the most haunting question, I asked myself, why did the ghost reach out and cross over from the Other Side, haunting me? Why did the ghost call me by the name 'Maribelle?'

I found myself caught living in two lifetimes at once: the present and the past. I was remembering bits and pieces to a past life while searching for the answers in my present life.

The ghost befriended and invited me into her haunting world. She granted me permission to photograph her mystical, ghostly images and wrote several letters to me revealing names and dates. I was the ghost's messenger and was given answers to help guide us into the new millennium.

The Childhood Dream

"Maribelle, Maribelle, Maribelle," a little girl's voice called out from beyond the white Southern mansion. The dream continued where I saw myself standing in a lovely tea rose garden. Fragrant yellowish-pink roses wilted in the summer heat. I gazed at my own reflection in the sea shell birdbath. The wind carried the perfumed petals gently falling down all round me. Some petals landed on my golden curls and others drifted along the water's edge. My purple hoop dress shimmered in the bright afternoon sun. An old magnolia tree stood cradling large white blossoms. The large branches were pulled down against the antebellium mansion's flat rooftop. The four towering Doric Greek columns stood majaestic on the front porch resembling Roman soldiers standing guard.

"Maribelle," as I looked up a small girl stepped out from behind the big magnolia tree, "Can you play?" she asked. The sunlight bathed her long auburn curls casting a soft glow on her rosy face. Her green eyes sparkled and her cheeks flushed from the summer's heat. Her white hoop dress was adorned with tiny embroidered roses. My dream ended there. I continued to dream about the little girl in the tea rose garden throughout the years. She continued to address me by the name Maribelle, but I did not understand why. She never told me her name.

In the summer of 1992, my husband John and I both worked as park rangers in Alaska. We enjoyed the outdoors and traveling to new places.That following autumn, John accepted a ranger job in the Okefenokee swamp in Georgia. We packed our belongings and moved down to the deep South. magnolia trees shaded the brick style houses surrounded the lush flower beds. Cherry trees and water fountains decorated the town's square. Beautiful historical mansions were reminders of the old South. We found the South an interesting place, enriched by its historic treasures.

Living in the South, I started to dream about the little girl. The setting was the same antebellium mansion where on the front porch stood the little girl. I was surrounded by a sea of white cotton fields. In the distance I heard a train whistle blow loudly. I walked down a dirt path to the many rows of antebellium mansions. I saw the little girl standing on the mansion's large front porch. She greeted me with a huge smile.

The little girl and I sat on a quilted blanket in the shade of a magnolia tree and played with our porcelian dolls. My doll had fine golden hair and blue eyes.

15

Her doll had auburn hair and green eyes. She told me her father's friend had brought the dolls back from his travels to France. We played tea time. The little girl and I sipped fresh squeezed lemonade from the rose pattern tea cups. We laughed and talked to our dolls. My dreams were surreal.

Two years had passed. We were living in a small log cabin in the swamp. On a lazy summer afternoon, I was awakened by the phone loudly ringing across the room. There stood the little girl at the foot of my bed. I was startled by how life like she was. I stared at her ghostly presence. She vanished into a misty haze. The phone call was news about my husband's job transfer to central Georgia.

The night before the moving truck was to arrive, I starred out the cabin window. From my bed, I heard a lonely whippoorwill sing out into the still night air. The spanish moss draping from the oak branches looked like ghosts in the moonlit night. I laid my weary head back on my pillow and started to dream again . . .

This time the little girl took my hand and led me down a dirt path deep into the forest. We came upon a white house on a grassy knoll. We peered through the front sun room windows on the left side of the house.

Inside, the walls were freshly painted white and the wood floors shined brightly. We stepped into the empty house and stood in front of the fireplace.

She smiled at me. I awoke to the alarm clock's buzzing .

That day John and I drove toward our new home. Tall pine trees lined the roadway as we turned off the main highway onto a paved road. The surroundings looked familiar to me as an anxious feeling overwhelmed me. In the distance, a dirt road led us to the white house on a grassy knoll. I jumped out of the car and ran to the left side of the house. The sun room was in full view. "Can you believe it?" I asked.

"Last night the little girl showed me this house in my dream" I said. I was beginning to realize the little girl was more than a dream; rather, a visitor from another place, another dimension, perhaps the place called the Other Side, from where the dead come and visit us.

The Folklore Ghost Sylvia

During the holidays, John and I drove to a small town called Eatonton in central Georgia. This town celebrated an old traditional custom during the Christmas holidays by decorating the historic district. As we drove by several beautiful grandiose mansions, a particular antebellum mansion looked very familiar to me. The bronze sign on the front of the mansion read "Panola Hall." The place looked haunted. Across the street was the town library, where I found several articles written about the mansion and its resident ghost called Sylvia. The articles documented the ghost sightings by several witnesses over the past one hundred and thirty years, and including the previous owners of Panola Hall Dr. Hunt and Mrs. Hunt.

One ghost story was recorded back in 1932, as written on the account of the town's librarian Miss Alice. One afternoon she bustled the school children into the library room that looked across the street into Panola Hall's front porch window. All eyes were on the ghost standing beside Dr. Hunt sitting in his reading chair. Miss Alice asked the children to tell her what they saw. One child remarked that Dr. and Mrs. Hunt had company. "Look at the pretty young woman wearing a white dress with long dark hair," a school boy pointed out. The librarian did not need anymore convincing that indeed, she had seen a ghost.

The two-story mansion has an appealing ambiance for the passerby. The building's simple design was to recall the Greek temples that influence many mansions built during the antebellum period. The long nine foot tall windows drew in a spectacular view.

A wealthy landowner Henry Trippe, in 1854, constructed the thirteen rooms Greek Revival mansion for his new wife. Lavish gardens were planted and sea shell birdbaths placed around the mansion grounds. They had two beautiful daughters: Mary and Louise. Rumors had; that tunnels were built under the mansion's basement to hide Confederate soldiers and stow away weaponry.

The townsfolk thought, perhaps, the ghost could have been one of the Trippe's daughters. The other story was a friend of the Trippe's family committed suicide after hearing tragic news about her sweetheart's death in the Civil War. The young girl threw herself off the second story balcony to her death.

The Trippe's descendants rented the house to a well-respected Dr. Hunt and his new bride, Louisa Prudden. The doctor named the mansion Panola Hall when he purchased the house in 1891 (In Choctaw, 'Panola' means cotton). Mrs. Hunt, childless, turned her creative energy to writing poetry. Dr. Hunt built a library right across the street for his wife, where her published works can still be found. In 1886, her husband improved the economy in Eatonton, by establishing the dairy industry. For his greatest contribution, he brought the rabies vaccine from France to Georgia. The couple was highly revered and well respected by the community.

Mrs. Hunt recalled first seeing the ghost at the top of the stairs. She was sitting and reading a book, when she heard laughter coming from the upstairs hallway.

Curious, Mrs. Hunt stood up and peered around the corner to see a young girl standing at the top of the stairs. "How dare you laugh at me in my own home,"she called out. The girl glided down the stairwell banister laughing. She disappeared into thin air. Mrs. Hunt stood in disbelief what had just happened. At first, Mrs. Hunt hesitated to tell her husband, but in no time at all, the pretty young ghost showed herself frequently to both Mrs. Hunt and her husband.

Mrs. Hunt

Mrs. Hunt was so taken with their new guest she named the ghost Sylvia. The ghost sightings continued long after the Hunts passed away. Although the ghost's identity remained a mystery, the townsfolk continued to call her Sylvia.

I photographed a ghost floating down the stairs.

My Visit To The Haunted Mansion

My journal read, "On this cold February morning, I took my first steps into the haunted house. Life as I had known, would be altered to another reality." How true those words rang .

On February seventh, I arrived at the front steps of the haunted mansion. I brought a camera and note-book to document any ghost sightings. I wore my crystal beaded necklace to clear any negative energies that may surround me. I visualized a white, bright light surrounding my whole being and said a prayer of protection. Haunted houses can host good and evil spirits at the same time.

Dr. Robert Lott graciously invited me into the haunted mansion. He had lived in a smaller house behind Panola Hall for the previous thirteen years. His dream was to restore the two story antebellum house to become his permanent living residence and have a medical museum in it.

He led me on a private tour around the thirteen rooms. A few furnishings and unpacked boxes were scattered throughout the empty rooms on the main floor. He showed me the front bedroom where the Hunts's had slept. A night stand, sofa, couch and oak chair furnished the large bedroom. Dr. Lott offered to brew a

fresh pot of coffee. "Make yourself at home," he called
out as he left the front door closed behind him. The
house was cold. I placed a vibrational energy around
my body. Tiny golden lights fluttered in a circle
around me. A wall of condensed energy formed
before my eyes. Slowly, the mansion became alive.

Up on the second story floor sounds of a little girl whistling drifted from the top of the stairs.

"Hello," I called out. My words vaporized in the chilled air. Ghostly activity revealed children's laughter and soft footsteps running on the second story floor above me. I held onto the wooden banister and climbed up the stairwell. High pitched noises echoed down the dark hallway. My heart pounded with every step, as I moved closer to the last room. I saw a foggy mist coming out from under the doorway.

Slowly, I turned the glass doorknob and opened the door to a brilliant light that shined off the ghost's body. She stood in front a marble fireplace. The roaring fire cast an amber glow on the oak and marble bedroom set. Pink wallpaper and tapestry draperies decorated the bedroom. The ghost was a beautiful young woman in her early twenties; her long white hoop dress trimmed in white lace and adorned with tiny embroidered roses. She wore a beautiful damask rose in her long auburn hair.

"Here you are at last," she said as her green eyes sparkled with joy.

"Oh, my sweet Maribelle, you have come back to me." She turned to the glass window and vanished into thin air.

Where she had been standing raindrops trickled down the window pane. The bare walls and empty fireplace were eerie reminders that the clock had stood timeless since the year 1864.

(Where the ghost had stood in front of the fireplace in the haunted bedroom.)

The ghostly scent of fresh roses and wisteria was all that remained in the saturated air of the haunted bedroom.

That night, I wrote in my journal about the ghost sighting. What did the ghost want from me? I smelled her ghostly perfume, a familiar blend of roses and wisteria. As her perfume clung to my thoughts, I wondered why the ghost called me by the name Maribelle?

Soon, as I drifted off to sleep, I heard someone whisper "Maribelle." I awoke and saw two glowing fluorescent ghosts at the foot of my bed.

The ghost gleefully floated toward me "Can you play?" she asked. Her face was golden and eyes bright. She drifted closer and closer to my face. I rubbed my eyes and noticed a large German shepherd sailing along next to the small girl. Her night gown was the same color as the dog's shiny white coat.

"Promise me you will come back to Panola Hall." Her tiny voice echoed through the dense air.

"Yes, I promise, I will visit you in the morning," as I watched the ghosts floating away on an iridescent cloud out my bedroom window.

That following morning, I phoned Dr. Lott who graciously welcomed me back to visit his haunted residence. I walked up to the mansion's front porch, "Good morning Dr. Lott. How are you?" I felt anxious about seeing the ghost.

"Oh fine. I worked the evening shift at the hospital." He unlocked and opened the front door to the haunted mansion. "Please call me Bob," he politely asked. We walked in the large sun filled entrance way. The morning sun shone on his boyish good looks that made him look years younger than his age. He was comfortable talking about the ghost and his years working on restoring the mansion. I sensed the ghost's loving presence around us.

"Can you imagine the history stored in this huge mansion? If only these walls could talk," Bob's voice echoed throughtout the large empty rooms.

Ghosts' hauntings happened in old places. I asked him, "what secrets do you think are hiding in this house?"

"No telling," he joked, "hey, let me show you the attic." We walked by the parlor, a dark foreboding shadow slowly moved across the pine floors toward me. Quickly, I looked away as I followed Bob up the stairs to the haunted bedroom.

I felt cool drafts and had an odd feeling that we were not alone. Our voices echoed as we entered the haunted room where the ghost had been seen by previous guests. My stomach felt queasy and my head started to spin. I saw illuminating tiny lights fluttering around in the open air.

Bob opened a small concealed door leading up to the attic. We stepped in the closet area and looked up to the rafters. I turned and looked down over my left shoulder. A white misty hazed covered the bedroom's front window, where, strangely, the outside green shutters remained closed, concealing any sunlight.

I watched as the ghostly form took shape. I did not say anything to Bob as we walked down the backstairs to the basement. "Here is the place where my guests have told me they have smelled the ghost's perfume," he said. There was an old musty smell lingering in the corner rooms where old junk piles and boxes had been stored over the years. From there Bob showed me his restoration project, sanding and painting the window shutters. He calls on his girl-friend to come down and work on the weekends. "She has been a big help to me restoring this place. Would you like to come by this weekend and meet her." "I would like that very much, may I bring my husband too?" I asked.

"That would be great." He smiled. "I need to go to town and run errands. You are welcome to stay here and look around the place. See you Saturday morning around eleven o'clock." He left and drove away in his truck.

I walked back inside the mansion. Alone now, I carried my camera to document any more ghosts' sightings. High-pitched noises whistled from the rooms on the top floor. I climbed up the stairs and stopped in my own footsteps. Down the dark hallway, I saw the little girl and the white German Shepard standing together. The ghost floated through the closed door. I loaded the film into my camera body. Slowly, I opened the bedroom door.

" May I photograph your ghostly image?" I asked the ghost. An euphoric feeling rushed through me as the ghost spoke, "My sweet Maribelle, see how high I can float up in the air! Oh, come and join me. Your doll waits for you." The ghost raised her white parasol umbrella over her audburn curls. I stood in the door entrance and photographed the ghostly scene.

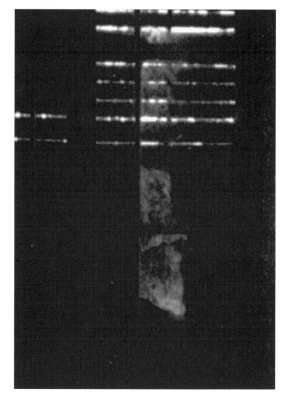

Above is the little girl and her dog floating
below the window shutters where light is coming through.

I rushed down the front porch's steps around to the left side bedroom windows. Where I looked up and saw the ghost peering out the clear window pane. She wore a white hoop dress and a damask rose in her hair. She stood and watched me from behind the glass and revealed the porthole in which she looked out into the outside world. At one time, not long ago, the world, where she too, had once lived.

The haunted window was a porthole to the Other Side.

"Sylvia" looking out the window

*The Phantom looking out upper
middle window pane.*

The ghost hand holding the Civil War soldier's tin type.

Little boy ghost looking out haunted window

Saturday afternoon my husband and I drive to meet Bob and his girlfriend. As we walked up the driveway we saw Bob place his arm around his girlfriend's waist. "Kathie, this is the woman I told you about who is interested in ghosts, and her husband is a park ranger."

The pretty woman stepped forward, "nice to meet you both," she said, as her bright blue eyes greeted us with warmth.

"Let's relax and enjoy the afternoon, we can visit and barbecue steaks," Bob suggested. We gladly accepted his invitation. John and Kathie drove to the market while Bob prepared the barbecue grill. The mansion's grounds looked inviting, so I took a walk around the old place.

A strange feeling overcame me. I stood under the magnolia tree beside an empty birdbath half buried in the green grass. The sweet smell of the magnolia blossom fragrance filled the air. I closed my eyes. "Maribelle, Maribelle, Maribelle," called a voice, all too familiar to me. "Yes, I am here," I whispered gently.

I opened my eyes. For a moment, I caught a glimpse of the tea rose garden.

Hauntings

This scene had replayed in my head since I could recall my childhood dreams. I remembered a little girl in the white hoop dress with auburn hair. Was this her home?

Had I been here too? How long ago? My attention was drawn to the balcony screen door opening and slamming shut. Chills ran down my spine.

Perhaps it was the breeze blowing through the mansion's top floor. I grabbed my camera and walked into the mansion. The front screen door closed behind me. Right away, I smelled a fragrant rose and wisteria perfume in the hallway. I followed the perfume up the stairs.

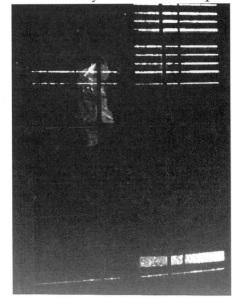

I saw a young woman in a white flowing dress. Brilliant rays streamed from her ghostly body.

"Oh, take my hand," the ghost reached out toward me. I stood paralyzed, watching her whimsical dance. She whirled around and around in a golden shower of lights. She tilted her head back and laughed.

I heard the front door slam shut on the bottom floor. I nearly dropped my camera. An eerie silence loomed around me in the haunted bedroom. I stepped up to the window and pressed against the square window pane. The surface was cool to the touch.

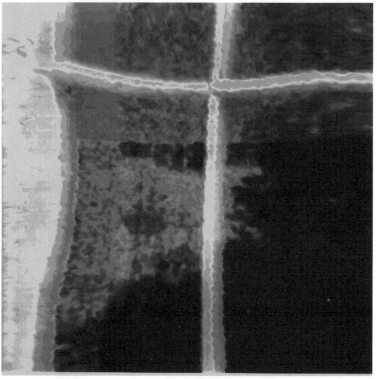

"How can one dimension of time change so rapidly?" I wondered. My handprint left tiny beads of sweat clinging to the clear window pane. A smaller impression of a handprint formed next to mine. The long bedroom window fogged over. Three words were scribble in longhand: joy, piety and harmony.

A sudden chill blew around my body. The cold sensation continued to move into the hallway. I was curious to see the other rooms from across the haunted bedroom. When I stepped into the empty room, dark shadows moved down the walls and forming into a black liquid substance that spilled out into the hallway floor.

 I felt an icy breeze moving closer to me. I tried walking down the stairs when the dark presence trapped me on the stairwell, pulling me down toward the parlor. Something chased me, as I rushed toward the open front screen door and ran out. My heart raced knowing something had tried to attack me.

I looked up through the second story window where the dark shadow had tried to attack me on the stairs. Slowly, the inside window panes turned solid black. A female ghost pressed her ghastly white face up against the window pane displaying her long fangs. Long black hair hung down around her pale white face and dark circles laid under her deep-set dark eyes. The phantom's black cloak covered the window. She tapped, tapped, tapped against the glass pane. Our glances locked.

I took out my camera and began to photographed the entity. Wondering what dark secret was hidden in the haunted mansion.

The phantom appeared in the middle window pane.
Her dark cloak caped below her eyes.
Other ghosts float above her.

I asked Kathie and Bob about seeing any ghosts. They had not encountered any ghosts. I showed both of them the ghost photographs. They were surprised and amused. Bob encouraged me to take more photographs and was amazed by my gift to see ghosts.

The lazy afternoon sun slipped away into nightfall. We said our goodbyes and our thanks. I gave my phone number to Kathie and asked her to call me whenever she was in town.

Beyond The Grave

That night, I wrote in my journal about the
ghost encounters, when an unknown presence auto-
matically took over my hand and scribbled out the
initials L.M.T. The following words flowed onto the
white paper "Maribelle, my dear cousin. Oh, how I
miss thee." I asked the loving presence in my room,
"what was my last name?"
The name McGehee was slowly and precisely written
on the paper. "What year was I born?" The pencil
scratched up and down a simple line, then round to
an eight and to a four and lastly, to a five. The num-
bers written were the year 1845. Chills ran down my
back. The name "Maribelle McGehee " haunted me. I
knew the name meant a passage into another lifetime.
My present life had crossed paths with the past. I felt
a very strong connection to the haunted house. I
wanted answers to the mystery of who I had been
and how I was a part of the ghost's life.

The Dolls

Georgia's small towns have the best antique stores. I found the ghost's dolls in an antique shop about twenty miles outside of Eatonton.

The sign read 'Antiques and Collectibles' outside a small red brick building. The hanging bell rang loudly as I pushed opened the storefront door. My eyes feasted upon hidden treasures scattered everywhere. I squeezed between the old furniture, glass lamps, stained glass windows, fireplace mantels, dishes, books and other items laid in open boxes on the wood floor. A burly middle age man yelled out from the back, "Let me know if you need any help."

My attention centered on an oak and glass china cabinet. I saw two porcelain dolls in the glass case that had a haunting resemblance to the dolls in my childhood dream. One had auburn hair and green eyes while the other had blue eyes and golden hair. I barely heard the man's voice, "Can I help you Miss?" asked the burly man. He interrupted my deep thoughts on the dolls and what they meant to me. My heart raced as I anticipated what the price of the dolls would be. I heard myself asked him, "Yes, I am intereted in these dolls?" I said as I stared in through the glass case.

He rubbed his hands together. "Let me see, these
porcelian dolls were handcrafted in France, I believe
around the year 1835." He opened the glass case and
carefully pulled out their porcelain bodies.

"How much are they?" I asked without hesitation.

He rolled his eyes upward as a figure came off the
top of his head. " Fifty dollars for both ladies." I felt
an overwhelming joy, and gladly paid him the money.
Finding the dolls was living proof that indeed a past
life had occurred between me and the ghost. I found
an important clue to the mystery about the ghost's
and my past lives.

43

The Visitor at The Cemetery

I poured myself a cup of fresh brewed coffee. The steam vapors floated upwards as I added cold half and half diluting the muddy black liquid. My sleeping patterns had been interrupted by waking up to the clock radio at exactly 5:00. The early birds were chirping loudly. I tried to fall back to sleep, but found myself crawling out of bed. Every morning I had been writing down my dreams and ghost sightings in my journal. That particular Friday morning, I opened the notebook and found the words, "go to the cemetery," scribbled in long hand across the paper. Was it a message from beyond the grave? Maybe it was a message to help me solve the puzzle about my past life. I was urgent to find out what the messenger wanted to reveal.

I parked my car under a shady tree in the cemetery. Stone graves stood and flat marble slabs laid in every direction as far as the eye could see. Perspiration dripped down my face and soaked into my tiedye t -shirt. The hot humid air was like a steam bath. "I cannot believe it's only ten o'clock in the morning." I mumbled to myself as the morning hours stretched out into a scorching afternoon.

Patiently, I waited to see who or what would come forth. A raven flew above me and landed on a cypress tree branch. The bird croaked loudly across the graveyard. I looked across the gravestones and saw a tiny young woman walking down the path. Her flowing auburn hair shimmered against the long black beaded dress. Strong gusts of wind moaned through the cypress branches as she walked past by me. Her porcelain face looked waxy. A gold locket hung below her beaded neckline. She carried a red rose and a small black book.

I watched as the ghost walked through the iron gate that stood two feet high around the grave site. She bent down at the foot of a grave and placed a single red rose onto the weathered marble slab. She opened her black book.

She glanced upward directly at me. Her mouth twisted and turned but I could not hear any words. I saw tears streaming down her ghostly face. Slowly, she disappeared into a white mist in the late afternoon shadows.

In the breeze the ravine's croaking sounded like a faint woman's voice calling out "Maribelle, Maribelle, Maribelle!" I felt an overwhelming sadness come over me. I slowly moved off the shaded seat and walked over to where she vanished into thin air. I pulled open the gate.

A beautiful red rose had been laid on the weathered grave. I kneeled down and held the fragrant flower. I swept away the dead Magnolia leaves uncovering the flat marble. The moss-covered slab had deep etched words that read the following name and dates; "Mary Elizabeth McGehee De Jarnette." She was born on January 31, 1838. and she died on June 15th, 1861. The ghost revealed to me a part of her past.

The ghost swept away any doubts that she indeed existed, and was coming forth stepping into my world, showing herself, and leaving behind a tangible clue; a person's name connecting the ghost's life to the past, and searching for her once again, in this lifetime.

Later that evening, Kathie called and invited me to sleep over on Saturday night. I accepted her invitation to spend the night alone in the haunted mansion. Saturday afternoon I packed my camera, film, spiral notebook, pencil, flash light, bottled water, toothbrush and sleepwear. Kathie would be spending the night in the smaller house behind the haunted mansion. I felt safe knowing that if something unexpected should happen, she would be near. Kathie opened the front door. I laid my day pack down and hugged her.

"Where's your other half?"I asked her. "Bob won't be back till late Sunday morning, so we have the place to ourselves. I have dinner on the stove and we can watch videos," she fanned herself. "You know the mansion is not well ventilated, all the windows are sealed shut." She then pulled opened the drawer and took out mansion's key. "Hey, let's put your overnight bag in the mansion" she said.

We walked over together to the haunted mansion. Kathie unlocked the front door. She showed me the front bedroom where the Hunts had slept. The room had a sofa bed and clean sheets lay on the oak chair. "The bathroom light is the only one that works in the house" she said, as she switched on the light fixture.

I noticed a candle and a box of matches sitting on the night stand. We closed the front door and walked along the path to the back house. The street lights cast ghostly shadows against the mansion. My thoughts drifted on the house being haunted. I felt anxious about spending the night all alone in such a big empty house.

Several hours went by and I was getting tired. I asked Kathie to walk with me over to the haunted mansion. I stumbled on the steps leading to the mansion's paved path, when a dog rushed out of the bushes and barked at us. My heart was racing. "He nearly scared me to death" I told Kathie.
The mansion's front door slowly creaked opened. "Good night," Kathie teased as she closed the front door. I pointed my flash light towards the hallway. The electrical cords dangled above the stairs and cast long shadows on the walls. "Well, here I am, at last" as my words trailed off into the complete darkness.

The bathroom light clicked off as soon as I finished brushing my teeth and washing my face. I fumbled in the dark room towards the sofa bed. The street lights casted light through the bedroom window. The large mansion was eerily quiet. I layed in bed and listened to the dead silence. The stale musty odor was suffocating me. I closed my eyes and drifted off to sleep.

Mystical Experince

I was awakened by a loud grandfather clock
striking at midnight. The twelve loud chimes echoed
throughout the mansion like church bells. My heart
pounded as I fumbled searching for the matchbox on
top of the night stand. "Everything is going to be
fine" I muttered to myself half scared and half awake.
The deafening noise abruptly stopped. I reached for
the matchbox and pulled out a single match, striking
it against the box. The candlewick burned slowly
absorbing the oxygen in the dense air. The candle
flame grew brighter and brighter. My eyes adjusted
to the dimmed light. I looked across to the oak chair
and saw a silhouette of a tiny woman. "Maribelle,"
She softly whispered in a child's voice as not to
frighten me. She wore a long pink nightdress. A
fragrant damask rose adorned her long auburn hair.
"Oh, how long we have been departed my dear sweet
cousin." She said.

She stood up and moved closer to me. Her ghostly
presence smelled like fresh roses and wisteria flowers.
I did not fear the ghost.

She reached out and took the candle holder. I
crawled out of the bed and walked toward her. We
stepped out into the open hallway.

Everything looked different. I was in a time warp dating back to the mid 1800's. The candlelight flickered brightly against the crystal chandelier that hung from the high hallway ceiling. Mirrors and family photographs hung on the pink papered walls. I noticed a blue ribbon hanging above a woman's portrait. The ghost showed me a portrait of a young woman. She spoke in a soft voice "This is my dear sister Mary, she loved to sit in the garden and do paintings of the roses. Mother mostly cherished Mary's devotion and work that she had done in the church."

Small gold leaves decorated a beveled mirror that hung on the wall. The ghost motioned me to come closer to gaze into the round mirror. I saw my own reflection standing next to her. My long brown curls flowed against my flushed high cheekbones. My eyes were crystal blue and red lips full. We were both wearing the same pink cotton nightdress.

Sadness overwhelmed me. I looked into the round mirror. White smoke like a heavy fog covered over our reflections. The mirror darkened and then became crystal cleared. I looked deeply into the mirror and saw a young woman bent over a boy who appeared to be sleeping. She wore a long black dress. I peered closer and saw her removing his blood stained clothing. She bathed his lifeless torn and bruised body. He was a small child.

She dipped her fingers into a small glass bowl. The young woman anointed the sign of the cross on his forehead as she held the child in her arms. The ghost faced me, "He is my youngest brother." She looked away from the sad memory. She could not hold back the tears streaming down her ghostly face.

"Oh, God helps us all. We turned our young boys into soldiers," she cried. "My brother wanted to join the company troops. I remembered hearing the train whistle blow. Our family learned the tragic news he was killed in the war. So many young boys and men returned home wounded or dead. Our country fought so long," she wept.

"The war has long been over" I spoke trying to comfort the ghost. In the dimmed candlelight her green eyes glassed over. The ghost's tiny young face showed her sadness and grief. For a long time had past where she could not escape her loss and longing. She was kept a prisoner in the old mansion. "So many families were torn apart by the war," she recalling the past scenes to me.

"The wounded and sick traveled long distances by train or covered wagons to hospitals. They were the lucky ones who survived to go back home to their families and sweethearts. Other soldiers were held captive and remained prisoners of war." she said, moving her hands to cover her face. "But Maribelle," she said, whatever happened to my Captain Dooly?"

54

The ghost was haunted by the Civil War and its lost tragedies. I wondered what had happened to her more than one hundred years ago?

I asked the ghost, "Were you the little girl in my childhood dreams?"

Her green eyes sparkled, "Yes, I was."

The ghost as a little girl peering out the window.

The Secret

We walked along the open hallway. I gazed at the beautiful oak and marble furnishings. Beautiful hand crocheted laces covered table tops. The walls were decorated with fancy french pink wall hangings. In the mansion's parlor and dining rooms, crystal candle chandeliers hung in the center of each large room. Gold ornate framed mirrors hung on the walls. The ghost led me up the stairs. I walked lightly as if I were floating on air.

A cold draft oozed out from the right side of the house. The bedroom doors remained tightly closed. We looked out the window at the top of the stairs as she spoke about her life.

The ghost said,"My father built cabins for all his Negro help out yonder in the fields. He taught us to cherish and be kind to those who were less fortunate and to respect those who helped us. Our family built a church for both white folk and Negro help to attend Sunday service. My Father gave his solemn word in a hand written promissory note to a field slave Jacob Henry to provide for his care, apprenticeship and to be paid as a free colored." I saw joy in her eyes as she spoke about the people who cared for her.
" My sweet cousin Maribelle, you traveled by train from Virginia."

The ghost's words triggered in me a past life memory. "Yes, I remember us playing with our porcelain dolls and admiring the tea rose garden. I have not forgotten when we sat by the bedroom window and listened to the Negroes singing spiritual hymns in the early evening down below in the Negro quarters," I said.

The ghost bent down and introduced herself to me, "My given name was Louise McGehee Trippe." The ghost stepped across the room and picked up a silver small frame off her oak dresser. She held out Mrs. Hunt's photograph.

"The Hunt's had given me the folklore name 'Sylvia.' I was the youngest daughter of Mr. and Mrs. Henry Trippe." She looked around the room at her collected treasures. "Yes, as a ghost, I collected things and brought them back to the Other Side. I have given gifts, as well, to the people that I have visited." The ghost was surrounded by many beautiful things from her past.

At that moment, my whole being was in the year 1864. My past life's memories were about to be revealed to me.

Louise carried the candle up to her bedroom. I saw one large bed and a smaller bed situated side by side. Roses were engraved on the oak bed frames. The blue china pitcher sat inside a larger bowl on the oak and marble night stand. Two crystal candle holders and a large square mirror sat on the mantel. An oil lamp was on the center of a square oak dresser and mirror.

I stared out the window. Purple and blue clouds drifted across the night sky. "Can I share a secret?" Louise asked me. "Close your eyes. Now open your eyes." I gasped in amazement at the large animal seated looking over the window sill.

"Oh, he is a lion!" I shouted. His long golden mane hung around his head and fell down his shoulders. "Yes. He is a lion" Louise said.
"Can I hug him?" I put my arms around his neck. I buried my face into the lion's soft fur. He purred very loudly. "Oh, he likes you" The ghost laughed. "He is my protector." "From what?" I asked.

Slowly, the ghost turned her head and looked away from the doorway. She pressed her tiny fingers up to my lips. A dark shadow wisped from under the closed door across the hall. The lion leaped forward at the shadowy cloaked figure that threatened to enter through the bedroom door. The room grew darker as the shape turned into a phantom. Her long black hair flowed down around her pale white skin. She turned and glared at me with her coal black eyes. She wore the face of death. "Do not look into her eyes." Louise calmly spoke. "She is pure evil."

Hissing at the lion, the phantom beared her fangs. Loudly, the lion roared showing his teeth. I shuddered in terror at the ghastly sight.

The phantom fled down the flight of stairs, the lion
laid down in retreat licking his paw.

The ghost staring out the window. The lion is standing
above her. His head can be seen above her's.

Reflections of The Past

"Louise, why do you stay here?" I searched for answers on her tiny delicate face. She pulled out a small silver box from the dresser drawer. She sat on the bed. Carefully, she opened the engraved silver lid and showed me what treasures were laying inside. In perfect order, she laid a wilted rose bloom, a lock of brown hair, a gold locket, a purple silk ribbon, a string of pearls, pink glass beads, butterfly wings, sea shells and letters. "My sweetheart's letters to me." She pulled out a small tintype. "This is my Captain Dooly" she said.

I held the tintype up close to look at the handsome face of a young man wearing a mustache.

"Oh, he has the softest brown eyes" I said.

See the hand holding tintype Civil War soldier above.

Sadness swept over the ghost's face. She grabbed my hand, "Maribelle, the time we shared during the civil war, you stood by my side. When my dear sister Mary was taken ill, her husband, even though he was a doctor, could not save her from the fever. " Remembering, she fondly held her sister's gold locket over her heart.

"Mary was twenty-three years of age when she left behind a son and an infant daughter. The war tore families apart. First, women faced becoming widows and then head of the household," she continued. "Their daughters lost their fathers and brothers, while the war took mothers' sons too. Women were left to raise young babies and children by themselves. Our mothers' spirits drew inner strength to rebuild and reshape the spirit of a nation," Louise said.

I closed my eyes and allowed the ghost's energy to flow through my body. I felt the warmth of her heart pounding in my chest. Our spirits intertwined into one deminsion of time. I saw storm clouds rolling along the open skies. I saw lightning striking below in the oak groves and heard the loud thunder rumbling on the wide green hills. I turned into a raven spreading my wings, swooping down to the fierce fiery cannon explosions. I flew over blue and gray uniformed soldiers sprawled in rows of shallow ditches. I landed on an oak tree branch upon a rocky hillside.

I saw two small frightened boys hiding under a large boulder. Hunger shaped their small faces into living skulls. Both boys cried out for their mothers. War had left many hungry and scared.

The ghost was no longer a ghost to me. I spoke to her in a young woman's voice, "We were together in a time that dated back more than a century ago in the year 1864. You were my distant cousin" I said.

Maribelle

The ghost reflected upon her sweet cousin Maribelle, who she adored as a childhood friend. We were two young women reliving a moment in the year 1864. A calm peaceful feeling came over me as the ghost embraced me.

The ghost and her dog out in the tea rose garden

The Phantom

The grandfather clock chimed loudly three times. I opened my eyes and blinked into the pitch dark. Standing in the hallway a suffocating feeling fell all around me. As my eyes adjusted to the darkness, shadows were moving around me. I saw white misty vapors formed into a mysterious beautiful young woman. She wore an Edwardian black silk skirt and a separate beaded bodice. Her dark beauty was spell bounding. "Oh, where is your cousin?" she spoke in a ghastly whisper.

Her voice grew cold, "Tell her bittersweet darling, I found joy in my immoral deed." She moved closer to my face. I stepped back into my bedroom, away from the deathly creature.

"Who are you?" I asked.

"Call me Anne" her breath gave off a foul smell.

"Tell precious Louise that I would not hesitate to do it all over again" a low eerie laugh rumbled from the corners of her mouth. "What did you do to her?" I asked.

My body leaned against the bedroom door. Her fangs rubbed against her bluish lower lip. The phantom moved closer to me, drawing my breath from the stale air. "I fed her the purple flower" she spoke in an evil tone. "Where is her nasty beast?" she scoffed. Her dark hair hanging over her deathly pale face.

"I do not know what you did?" I said. "Tell me what you know" as my voice trembled.

"Maribelle, you left behind your sweet cousin and went off to travel across yonder. Louise was stranded and lost without you. I came to visit her and stayed. We were all frightened of General Sherman's troops." She laughed in an evil high pitch. "My plan worked so easily. I crushed the poisonous four petal purple flowers into a liquid. I put the serum into a tiny glass vile, adding a few drops to a small cup of tea, daily for a week. Your precious darling slowly wilted away," she confessed.

The phantom's face was dark gray, a white outline transformed her face into a death mask. Her dark eyes vented evil as steamy vapors rose off her ghastly body. She hissed as she slipped back into the dark shadows.

1854 Panola Hall, Eatonton Georgia

(a private residence)

Bessie

Stepping back into the bedroom, I crawled into the bed. Knowing I was protected from the phantom sitting in the parlor. She would not dare come into this room.

I wondered, "why did the phantom poison Louise?"

Looking out the bedroom window, there stood the ghost and lion under the night sky watching meteorite showers. The meteorites' long blazing tails streamed across the open night skies like fireworks on fourth of July. For an instant, the meteorite streaks across through the present and then in an instant disappears into the past.

"How can I help the ghost?" I questioned myself. Louise stood quietly in the doorway. Swarming around the room were tiny golden fireflies ."You were sent here on this night to recall your past life. Tell me what you remember. Tell me what was in your heart, in your spirit, in your soul," she asked. The ghost laid beside me on the bed.

I watched as the fireflies bounced up and down in the open room. My memories were deeply buried in the past.

"Oh, Louise, I saw us together as children playing in the tea rose garden. We were carefree young spirits without prejudice, and we did not understand why the war broke out." My words ended as I struggled to stay in the past. The ghost softly spoke, "Our fathers struggled with identifying life and its worth. With claims a white man's God-given right to own another child, woman, and man. Men bought and sold human beings into slavery." Louise held her hand up and motioned the fireflies to swarm in a circle around our heads. Their fluorescent wings tapped gently against us. "I remember your sweet mammy Bessie singing her ancestral mother's songs. Her wisdom helped us through our struggles. She spoke about the wind spirit carrying African tribal songs to her stolen children," I said.

Those words beat strongly in my heart as I felt Bessie's spirit stirring when I recalled the past.

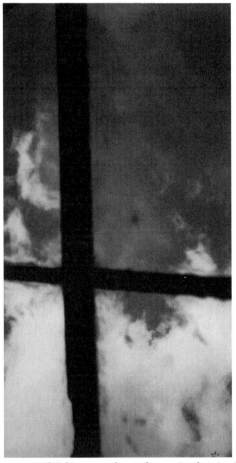

The ghost and I listened to the wind stirring through the magnolia trees, rustling their green broad leaves. We watched as Bessie's ghost floated in through the bedroom window. The winds calmed down to a soothing breeze. Bessie's spirit body turned into a halo. Her ghostly body illuminated golden rays.

I saw a beautiful Negro woman whose brown eyes were the color of golden honey and her soft dark skin the color of sweet molasses. She wore a white cotton turban and a sky blue dress. The ghost stood up and embraced Bessie. "We have waited so long to be together. Oh, Bessie we want to hear your story," Louise said. We sat on the bed and waited for her to speak.

Bessie's voice stirred my past life memories as she began "So long ago, the wind spoke to me. Oh, soothe our wearied spirits," Bessie closed her eyes and tilted her head as if she were listening to the wind. "Ah, I listened to my ancestors' wisdom; their words breathe new life into my weary bones as the wind carried fragrant breezes to sooth my spirit that longed for my lost family." She held a crystal walking staff." I was a young girl bought and sold into slavery. My home-land was a place far, far away. The slave ship sailed and carried human cargo across the seas to another continent thousands of miles away from my family. I was auctioned off to a man who was called Prince and lived on the coastal port town of Savannah. Then the man loaded me and other bought slaves into a train box. The train ride was hot and dusty before we reached the auction house in Milledgeville."

(Slave ghosts)
The words written on the right window pane are
Maribelle, joy and harmony.
The two slave ghosts are in the middle window panes.

Bessie calmly spoke, "Louise your father bought me at auction for one hundred dollars. So long ago, as a young girl, I had dreams too," Bessie whispered in an old woman's voice.

"My dreams were stolen. But choosing to empower myself, no one has the power to take away my free spirit." She placed her hand up against the window. The glass porthole opened into a colorful swirled showing us a wild safari where zebras and giraffes ran across the opened grasslands.

Bessie spoke in a powerful voice, "The most courageous animal was the lion that roamed freely in my birthplace and homeland called Africa. Within me I carried the lion's spirit. I did not allow the negative forces and hatred to breed into my heart." She held her hand over her heart.

"My heart was freed to love. I reached deep within my spirit to dream and hope for a brighter future. I passed on the lion's spirit to my own daughter Jezibele," Bessie's pride alive in her eyes.

"Jezebele was born a slave but Louise's father had given her the promise to be a free colored. She was a house servant in the mansion, where she was earning wages and learning to read." Bessie turned to me, "You were sent here to the Other Side, to help Louise. Not knowing how she died, kept her spirit trapped here in this house," she said.

74

"Maribelle, now is the time to help Louise by finding the clues to her mysterious death." Bessie pointed to the window that was blazing into spectacular reds and oranges. I gazed out the window as the fireball grew more brilliant.

Bessie spoke, "Maribelle, the spirit world has given you a rare gift. This gift will give you the chance to spend a few precious hours with Louise and help set her haunted spirit free, so she can leave behind the sad memories and go on to find peace."

Bessie turned to the blazing window, her ghostly body floated out the window and disappeared into the brillant African sunset.

The lion stood up and affectionately brushed up against Louise. He looked at her once more and roared loudly before jumping through the swirling colorful glass porthole. The ghost and I watched the lion's body disappear into the setting sun's amber glow casting over the wild safrai.

We watched the skies darken, as the lion's dark silloutte faded away. A tear trickled down the ghost's face. She was happy and yet sad that her long time companion was gone forever.

The ghost wanted to be freed too.

The Past Haunts The Present

"Remember" I said, " how we cried and hugged one another at the train station? I promised to write you on my travels across the country." That was all I could remember until meeting the phantom tonight. The ghost knew that behind the dark shadows loomed an evil presence.

"What did the phantom say to you?" Louise asked.

"The phantom's words spoke the truth about me leaving you," I said. Louise's eyes met mine. Sadness washed over her face as she spoke, "Maribelle, how much I missed you. Shortly, after you had left, a young woman who lost her family in the war came to stay with us. The war was moving closer towards Atlanta. Many families had moved down to stay in safer places. Our home was opened to folk in need." I interrupted the ghost, "Was her name Anne?" I asked? "Yes," she said as the ghost described the young woman's features. "She had long dark hair hung down around her pale face. And her dark eyes were cold. Bessie warned me that the young girl possessed a bad spirit. She told many lies. Strangley I had found my silver box had been opened. Because Anne had no family and no place to go, I felt sorry for the poor girl. I never told a soul what I thought about her.

Because our main worry was how much longer we could keep the warfare out of our homes. The war had already taken its toll on my family. I buried my sweet sister Mary to the fever, my uncles and brothers returned scarred forever by the war." She sighed.

Gazing down at her ruby and diamond engagement ring, the ghost said, "I worried about this house and the women's safety. For most men had been gone fighting over the years and many died in the war. The summer's heat was cooled by the constant rains. My memory recalled that the rain continued to fall. I had thought the mail stopped bringing Captain Dooly's letters on the account of the wet weather turning the dirt roads into mud pools. On my approaching dear wedding day, I received word about his whereabouts. Quickly the news spread about his capture. He had been in a great battle and taken a prisoner of war. A great pain stuck in my heart. I cried and prayed all night long that this could not be true. Every day, news traveled while General Sherman's troops marched closer to our homes. I was terrified of what would happen to my family. No one could escape a madman's death march." The ghost paced around the room as she continued to tell me her story.

"In the afternoons, Anne and I sipped our tea in the parlor. She was needlepointing purple flowers on her tapestry. Meanwhile the girl hummed to herself a low eerie tune. I was sitting at my mother's desk writing letters to you and the Captain. Sometimes, I caught a glimpse of Anne staring out the window muttering words to herself.

One evening, I sat close by, and overheard her say, 'death shall come to you.' I thought the girl had gone mad. Those dreadful words cannot escape my thoughts." Louise said.

A cold sweat rushed through my body as I relized that Anne was indeed the phantom who had poisoned the ghost.

Louise turned and walked towards the doorway. She stood looking away from me. "Maribelle, I could not keep up my strength. My body ached and my lungs were heavy. Bessie cooked a pot of her special remedy soup. My strength grew weaker and weaker by the day. Anne brought me a cup of her fresh brewed tea. She sat by my bedside and read to me. I was not able to eat. The rain was miserable and kept a cold dampness throughout the house. Everyones spirits were low. I was laying in my bed when we heard the news that Sherman and his soldiers were battling up in Atlanta" she quietly spoke.

"When Anne heard the news, she became hysterical. She went running through the bottom floor and up the stairs to the top floor and down the hall to my bedroom. Her face was frightfully pale and her dark eyes piercing as she stood in the doorway. Trembling, Anne spoke, 'I hope death shall come to you soon!' She screamed as she turned running down the hall to the balcony, where she jumped over the balcony's railing and fell to her death.

A few days later, Bessie sobbed as she told me the whole truth about Anne. 'Listen Louise, upon Anne's suicide, we received a message from her distant relatives, telling us the tragic news that Anne had poisoned her whole family. God only knows what she had done to you.' I can remember how Bessie sat over me crying knowing I was dying." The ghost stood quietly and stared out the window.

Death

The ghost was not happy being left behind far away from her dear lost sister Mary, whom she missed so much. She wanted their graves to be side by side. "In Mother's last testimony will, she gave Mary a beautiful memorial gravestone, but I was not to be buried next to my sister. Sixteen years later, my dear parents passed away and were buried together in the church cemetary." The ghost's face looked so sad and lost being without her sister.

I stood between two worlds: the past and the present. My past life was given back to me for a brief moment, so I could rescue the ghost.

I was about to reveal Anne's evil deed that caused the ghost's untimely death and trapped her spirit behind the mansion's walls. Most importantly, I wanted to tell the ghost she had the will power to set herself free.

"Louise, you are kind and honest. I want to tell you the truth about Anne's plot. She poisoned you. She was responsible for your death." The ghost took a deep breath and asked me, "Why would Anne do such a horrible deed?"

Anne's ghost remained hidden in the mansion's shadows. " She slipped the poison in your afternoon tea by adding drops of nightshade flower tincture. Her evil deed lead to her madness and turned her into a phantom," I said. Sadness filled in the ghost's haunted eyes.

"On my deathbed, I prayed to God, to keep our house safe from the soliders. I saw my lifeless body lay motionless on my bed as death slowly drained my last waking breath.The clock chimed five times, on that early morning, late in the month of October. My sweet mother placed the black mourning cloth on the clock and the bedroom's drapes remained closed. Bessie picked beautiful tea roses from the garden and sprinkled the fragrant petals across my lifeless body. I saw a brilliant white light and heard my sister Mary's voice calling out for me. But I could not leave. I stayed to protect the house from General Sherman and his troops. I loved this house and the tea rose garden. I dearly loved my father and mother who were God loving people. And I loved my sweet mammie Bessie and all that she taught me." She longing recalled.

Lessons and Blessings

"Louise, the war is over," I told her. "You can go now and be at peace."

The ghost placed her tiny hand over my heart. "What I gave was the goodness from my heart. I am ready to leave now, but how?" She questioned.

"The war's horrible tragedies have been long gone. Time has healed old wounds and given hope to allow the human spirit to grow new wings," I said.

The ghost in the far left lower window panes looking out.

"But I remain trapped by my memories and grief," Louise spoke in a haunting sad tone. "The war changed our families forever. I experienced a great deal of loss and sadness." The ghost bent her head down as she spoke, "I remembered Bessie's wise words, 'Remember do not let the past tragedies shape your current life's energies. The past is the past.

Story telling, writing, singing, art, breathes new life into the past events. Life is a gift. Every day shall be cherished. Take life and live it to the fullest. What truly matters is what comes from the heart.' Bessie words gave me enlightment and encouragement allowing my heart to remain opened." She said.

"Look, I can see the early morning dawn," I said. We stood together looking out the window as the sun rose over the horizon.

The ghost softly whispered, "I watched as the clouds danced along the winds while the winds soothed the trees. The trees grew and gave us cool breezes. The cool breezes gave us the air we needed to sustain life. This was how the divine spirit and the human heart intertwined to give us hope: that one day, all mankind may have a better understanding. To love our neighbor as thyself; to love ourselves first for who we are, and not to judge others for who they are not. All we can do is pray and hope for tolerance so the spirit may soar and grow inside of our hearts," Louise said.

"Yes, I said "its finding joy within, loving ourselves and growing wings so our spirit can fly. Every day we wakeup to the gift of life, to find joy and love. So we may renew our spirit."

The ghost broke out into a huge smile. We laughed as our voices spoke the same words in the same breath, "That unconditional love carries and feeds the spirit. The spirit nurtures and brings peace to the soul. Love energizes and dignifies a person's life. God's teachings spread joy, piety and harmony to live life as one."

We stood and smiled at each other. We became one in kindred spirits. We were one in the heart, the spirit, and in the soul. The love we felt for one another was cherished and remembered.

"Louise, it's time to leave behind the past and walk away from this place," I said. A foggy mist swirled around our astral bodies as I gently let go of her hand. The ghost stood gazing out the window for one last time. I watched her body fading away into the mist as I spoke to her, "go and set yourself free."

A bright light shining through the clear window pane awakened me.

I opened the front door and stepped out onto the front porch. Lingering around me was a faint smell of Louise's perfume of roses and wisteria in the morning air. A cool breeze was blowing through the trees. When I noticed a beautiful tiny bluebird sitting in the old magnolia tree.

Her song brought joy to my heart as I listened to her beautiful melody pouring out into the open air.

My spirit soared as I watched the bluebird fly away. I softly whispered, "Good-bye Louise."

The ghost sitting on the mantle.

Book orders: ghostlady@mindspring.com
or write to: The Ghost Lady
P.O. Box 131
Juliette, Ga. 31046

Book price $11.95 plus tax and shipping.

Hello,

I would love to hear from you. Please write to me about your ghosts stories. I would be interested hearing any ghosts' experince that you may had.

Happy Hauntings

The Ghost Lady

Please take note:

Panola Hall

is

a

PRIVATE
RESIDENCE

It is not open to the public

Thankyou